W9-DEE-614

CRUSHED!

Explore forces and use science to survive

Richard and Louise Spilsbury

A⁺
Smart Apple Media

Published by Smart Apple Media, an imprint of Black Rabbit Books
P.O. Box 3263, Mankato, Minnesota 56002
www.smartapplemedia.com

Published by arrangement with Watts Publishing, London.

Cataloging-in-Publication Data is available from the Library of Congress
ISBN: 978-1-62588-145-8   (library binding)
ISBN: 978-1-62588-396-4   (paperback)
ISBN: 978-1-62588-579-1   (eBook)

Printed in the United States by CG Book Printers
North Mankato, Minnesota

PO 1723
3-2015

Picture Credits
Dreamstime: Kapu, Neotakesu; Shutterstock: anshar, djgis, Jerry Sanchez, Maxim Petrichuk, Natali Snailcat, Paul Stringer, posscriptum, PRILL, Sven Scheffers, vadimmus, Wansfordphoto, Wollertz.

Bold words in the text are included in the glossary

WHO'S WHO?

JESS

Jess is a bit of a daredevil. She's always first to try something new. She loves skateboarding, climbing, and adventure stories.

BEN

Ben is a bit of a gadget fanatic. He carries his backpack with him at all times and it's full of useful—and not so useful—stuff.

AMELIE

Amelie is a science whiz. She's not a know-it-all, but she often has the right answers. She doesn't like getting her clothes dirty and her hair messed up.

ZAC

Zac is the youngest and although he never wants to be left out, he can get a bit nervous and is easily spooked.

CONTENTS

SNOWBOARDS AT THE READY

"I'm not so sure snowboarding is a good idea after all," says Zac nervously. "That slope looks steep."

"We'll practice on this flat area first. You'll love it once you get going," insists Jess.

"Easy for you to say," grumbles Zac.

"Well, I'll just be happy if I can stand up on my board for a bit," says Amelie. "Give me a push off will you, Ben?"

"Just go—you'll be fine. Some of us are getting cold here, waiting for you!" complains Ben.

"No, if someone gives me a big push I'll go further," insists Amelie. "Pleeaase!"

WHAT DO YOU THINK?

Amelie says being pushed hard will make her go further.

Is she right?

PROVE IT!

Explore pushing forces. You need:

| three toy cars | measuring tape

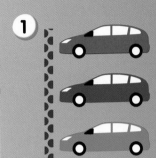

1 Line up three toy cars on a flat, smooth surface such as a wooden floor or a long table. To make it a fair test, the cars should all be the same type and size and should start from the same line.

2 Give one car no push, the second car a slight push and the third car a really hard push.

3 Measure how far the three cars go. Which car went furthest? Why do you think that is?

WHY IT WORKS

Forces are pushes and pulls, and can make things speed up and slow down. All forces have a direction. Pushes move things forward. In this activity, the cars are at rest until your pushing force acts on them. Amelie is right! The bigger the force used, the more the car will move and the further it will go.

SUPER STUNTS

"Wow, how does she do those amazing jumps? She's doing two full spins up there!" cries Amelie, watching in admiration as Jess spirals confidently through the air on her snowboard.

"The real question is—why does she do them?" sighs Zac.

"I wish I could do it," says Ben. "But I'm heavier than her, so I'd come crashing down to earth before I had a chance to try it."

"No," says Amelie. "You might be heavier than her but you're pretty much the same shape and size so you'd land at the same time."

"That sounds ridiculous," says Ben. "You can't be right this time, Amelie."

PROVE IT!

Investigate falling objects. You need:

❙ four small containers of the same size and shape, such as empty candy boxes
❙ four objects of different weights such as a marble, a feather, some cotton balls and a paper clip
❙ two friends

 Put one object in each container and close up all the containers.

 Ask two friends to stand at the top of some stairs or on chairs and hold the sealed containers at the same level and in the same position.

Do a "3-2-1-GO" countdown so that your two friends drop all four containers at exactly the same time. What happens?

WHAT DO YOU THINK?

Ben is right, heavier things always fall fastest.

OR

Amelie is right, objects of different **weights** that are identical in shape and size will land together.

WHY IT WORKS

Gravity is a force that acts at a distance, pulling things down. It keeps us from floating off into space and makes things you drop fall to the ground. Gravity exerts the same pulling force on all falling objects. Amelie is right! Things that are the same shape and size fall to the ground at the same time, even if one is heavier than the other.

AVALANCHE!

Suddenly, a deafening noise interrupts their conversation. A group of snowmobiles is racing across a ridge of snow above them.

"That's dangerous," says Zac. "The weight of those snowmobiles could break off that ridge of snow and start an **avalanche**."

"You're always worrying," Jess replies reassuringly. "It'll be fine."

"Don't speak too soon," shouts Ben. "Look!"

"Run!" yells Amelie, as they hear a dreadful cracking noise. An avalanche of snow starts to slide dangerously down the mountainside towards them, throwing up a blinding plume of white powder ahead of it...

?

WHAT DO YOU THINK?

Is Zac right, can extra weight cause things to fall off a ledge?

PROVE IT!

Investigate weight and gravity. You need:

⌐ long piece of cardboard
⌐ empty box or carton
⌐ chair
⌐ weights, such as coins

1 Bend the cardboard so there is a flat space at the top, and a slope. Rest this on a chair so the slope reaches the ground.

WHY IT WORKS

Weight is the pull of gravity on objects. The weight of the coins adds to that of the box. **Friction** resists the force of gravity, but when there are more coins in the box the force of gravity is greater than the force of friction, so the box begins to move. On the mountain, the extra weight of the snowmobiles causes the avalanche.

2 Rest the empty box or carton at the top of the slope with an edge hanging over, but so it feels well balanced.

○ Now put weights into the box on the side that is hanging over the edge. Put one coin in at a time. What happens?

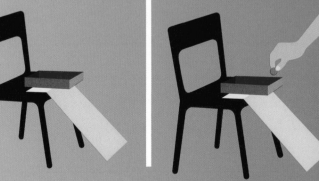

BURIED

Jess, Zac, and Ben wipe their eyes clear of snow and look round for Amelie, who is no longer beside them. They spot her—half-buried under snow, with her leg pinned down by a fallen tree.

"Oh no, Amelie! Are you OK?" they all shout, running towards her.

"Yeah, I think so," says Amelie. "Being caught in that avalanche was like being tossed about in a giant clothes dryer! Get this tree off me, will you?"

"But it's too heavy for us to lift," says Ben.

"Lay a branch over that rock to make a **lever** to lift the tree. The rock will be the **fulcrum**, the point around which the lever turns," instructs Amelie.

"The rock is too close to you. We need to roll it further away," says Jess.

"No, it'll work best closer to the tree we want to lift," insists Ben.

"Do something!" cries Zac. "Before Amelie freezes to death!"

WHAT DO YOU THINK?

Is Ben right? Is it true that the closer a lever's fulcrum is to the **load**, the less **effort** is needed to lift the load?

PROVE IT!

Experiment with moving a lever's fulcrum to see how it affects the effort needed to lift a load.

You need:

I a footlong ruler (30 cm)
I pencil
I tape
I two paper cups
I pebble, or other weight
I coins (all the same type)

1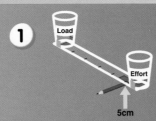

Label one cup "Load" and the other "Effort." Stick the cups to opposite ends of the ruler. Put the pencil under the ruler, below the 2 inch (5 cm) mark. Tape the pencil to the table.

2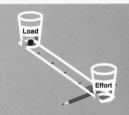

Place the pebble in the Load cup. Add coins to the other cup, one by one, until the Load cup is raised up. Make a note of how many coins are in the Effort cup.

3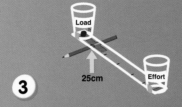

Empty the cups and do the test again, but with the pencil placed at 6 inches (15 cm) and 10 inches (25 cm). How did the position of the fulcrum affect the effort needed to lift the load?

WHY IT WORKS

Levers are **simple machines**, with only two parts, that are used to increase force. The "arm" of the lever is the part that you push or pull. The point around which the lever turns is called the fulcrum. Some levers help to lift heavy loads—the load is the object you are trying to lift. The effort is the force you use to push down on the lever to lift the load. Ben is right: when using a lever, the closer the fulcrum is to the load, the less effort is needed to lift the load.

SLIDING ALONG

"That's better!" sighs Amelie, once the tree is lifted. "But my leg hurts a lot. I don't think I can walk."

"What are we going to do?" worries Zac. "It's a long way back to the village and it'll be dark soon."

"I've got some rope in my pack," says Ben. "We'll tie branches together to make a sled." When they finish the sled and Amelie sits on it, it's very difficult to pull along.

"The problem is **friction**, because the sled is too rough," says Jess.

"She's right!" says Amelie. "If you make the sled from branches that are smooth, there will be less friction between the sled and the snow."

"Let's put the snowboards on the bottom. Then it'll slide down this slope easily," suggests Ben.

"Right—let's do it!" says Jess.

? WHAT DO YOU THINK?

Is Ben right? Will there be less friction with the smooth snowboards than with the rough branches?

14

PROVE IT!

Investigate how friction changes between surfaces when one of them is rougher or smoother. You need:

- small empty plastic pot with two holes in the top on opposite sides (ask an adult to make the holes with scissors)
- big box of cereal (securely closed)
- string about 3 foot (1 meter) long ● tape ● table
- small mat or piece of carpet
- coins or marbles
- piece of bumpy cardboard

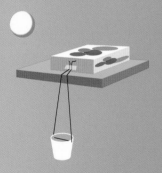

Tape one end of the piece of string to the end of your cereal box. Thread the other end through the two holes in the empty pot, and then tape that end to the cereal box, too. Lay the box on the table and dangle the pot over the edge.

Put coins or marbles into the empty pot, one at a time. How many does it take to make the cereal box move?

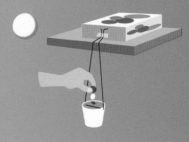

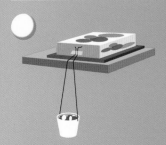

Repeat the test with the mat and then the bumpy cardboard underneath the cereal box on the table. What do you notice?

WHY IT WORKS

There is less friction between some surfaces than others, and the effects of friction can be reduced by changing the surface of one of the objects. Objects with rougher, bumpier surfaces create more friction. Ben and Jess are right: smoother objects and surfaces create less friction.

ESCAPE FROM WOLVES?

"What's that noise?" yells Zac, as a blood-chilling howl echoes through the air. "It sounds like wolves. They must be following us!"

"You're crazy," says Amelie. "There are no wild wolves around here."

"Well, maybe they escaped from a zoo," shouts Zac. "I'm not waiting to find out."

"We do need to go faster," says Jess. "It's getting windier and colder. Now that we're on flat land, let's make a sail from my dress so the wind can help us along."

"No, that's too small," says Ben. "We need something bigger, like the blanket in my backpack."

? WHAT DO YOU THINK?

Is Ben right? Does the size of a sail help an object move faster?

PROVE IT!

To investigate, you need:

I toy car I clay I skewer or chopstick I paper or cardstock
I scissors I tape I battery-operated fan or hairdryer

Put a blob of clay on top of the toy car and stick the skewer or chopstick into it.

Cut out some sails in different sizes. Tape one sail to a chopstick.

Put the car on a smooth, hard floor and blow it with the fan or a hairdryer on the lowest setting. Record the time it takes the car to travel 5 feet (1.5 m). Repeat with different-sized sails.

WHY IT WORKS

Moving air creates a force that moves in one direction. When it touches a moving object, it pushes against it. This is called **air resistance**. Air resistance increases with **surface area**. Ben is right: sails with a larger surface area produce greater air resistance and go faster and further.

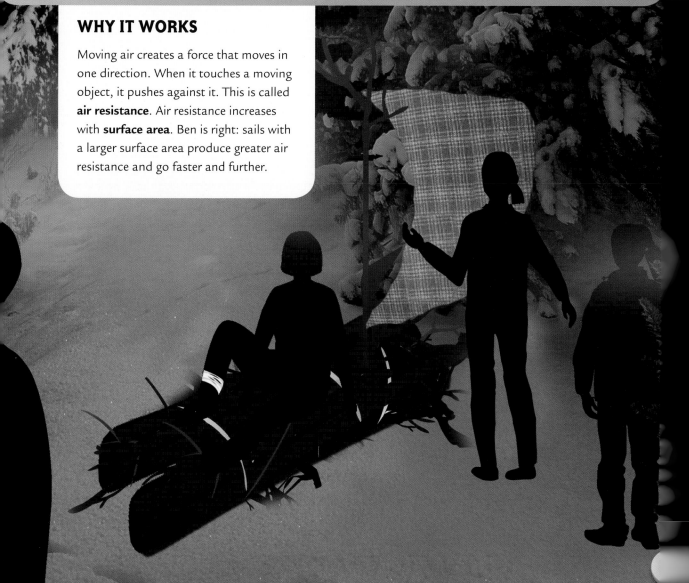

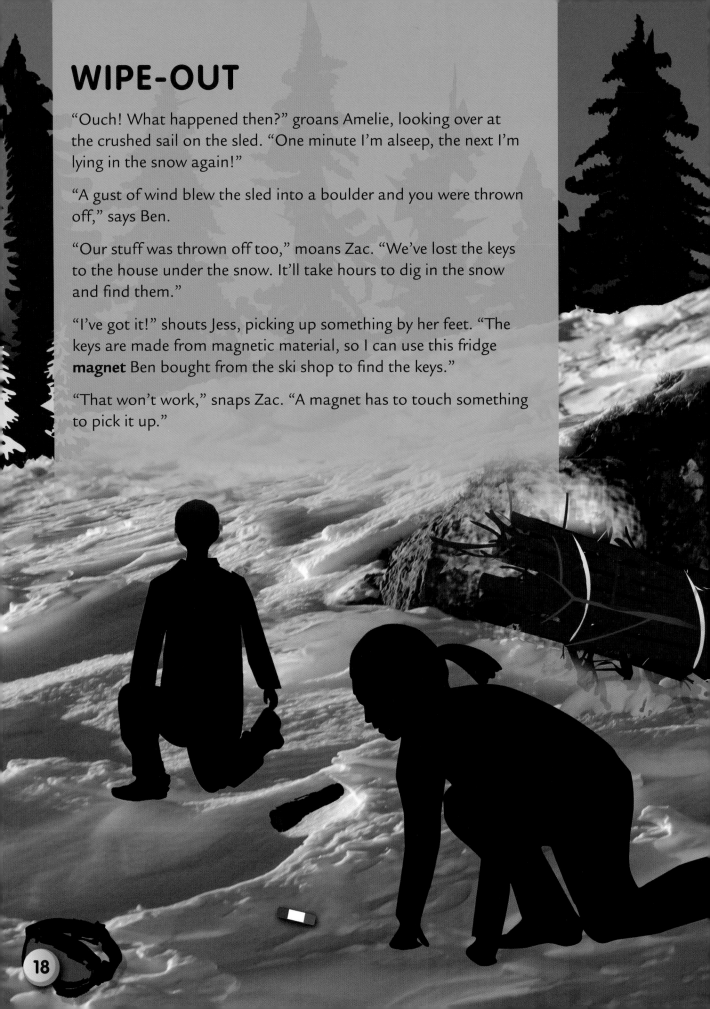

WIPE-OUT

"Ouch! What happened then?" groans Amelie, looking over at the crushed sail on the sled. "One minute I'm alseep, the next I'm lying in the snow again!"

"A gust of wind blew the sled into a boulder and you were thrown off," says Ben.

"Our stuff was thrown off too," moans Zac. "We've lost the keys to the house under the snow. It'll take hours to dig in the snow and find them."

"I've got it!" shouts Jess, picking up something by her feet. "The keys are made from magnetic material, so I can use this fridge **magnet** Ben bought from the ski shop to find the keys."

"That won't work," snaps Zac. "A magnet has to touch something to pick it up."

? WHAT DO YOU THINK?

Jess is right, magnets can work at a distance.

OR

Zac is right, magnets only pull on things they touch.

PROVE IT!

You can test if and how well magnets can pull on or attract things.
You need:

I strong bar magnet
I ten metal paper clips
I ten sheets of paper

Put the paper clips on top of one sheet of paper and move the magnet around underneath them. Does the magnet make the paper clips move?

Repeat, but add a sheet of paper and keep adding more sheets of paper until the magnet stops moving the paper clips. How many sheets did it take?

WHY IT WORKS

Jess is right: magnets can pull on things from a distance and even through some materials, such as paper or snow. The pulling force gets weaker across larger distances, which is why the magnet stops working through many sheets of paper.

A FOG DESCENDS

"Great. We found the keys but now we can only see a few steps ahead of us. Where did this fog come from?" complains Zac.

"I don't know—and no, we don't need a scientific explanation of fog right now, thank you Amelie!" snaps Jess, glaring at Amelie.

"I wasn't going to say that!" protests Amelie. "I was going to suggest we make a **compass** using the magnet and a needle."

WHAT DO YOU THINK?

Is Amelie right, can you make your own compass from a needle and magnet?

PROVE IT!

Make your own compass. You need:

I plate or saucer I water
I magnet (with north and south
ends marked)
I thin slice of cork from a bottle stopper
I sewing needle (be careful with this)

Stroke the north end of the magnet
(marked N) against the needle about
50 times. Always stroke in the same
direction, towards the sharp end.

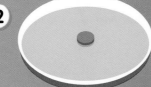

Fill the plate with water, and float
the cork on top of the water.

Gently rest the magnetized needle
on the cork. The cork will turn,
and the sharp end of the needle
will point towards the north.

WHY IT WORKS

The Earth acts as if it has a
magnet inside it with two
ends, one at each **pole**.
One magnetized end,
or pole, of your needle is
attracted to Earth's North
Pole. This end must be the
needle's south pole, because
opposite poles attract.
In the same way, the north
pole of a magnet points to
the south end of the Earth's
magnet—the South Pole.

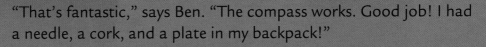

"That's fantastic," says Ben. "The compass works. Good job! I had
a needle, a cork, and a plate in my backpack!"

"Yeah, OK," says Jess. "There's no time to hear about your amazing
backpack again. Let's use this compass to find our way through this
horrible fog towards home."

"I'm with you, Jess!" says Zac.

TOO FAR TO GO?

"My leg is really hurting now," says Amelie. "And it's swelling up. Are we nearly there yet?"

"Well, now that the fog has cleared I can see the village, but this sign says we're still 6 miles away," replies Ben.

"We'll never make it back before dark," says Zac, biting his lip nervously. "We won't be able to see where we're walking. We could fall into a hole, walk into a wolves' den, anything!"

"We've told you—no wolves here!" says Jess angrily. "I'll figure out how long it'll take us to get there by timing Ben pulling Amelie along this next stretch."

"We haven't got time for games," says Zac. "How's that going to help us?"

WHAT DO YOU THINK?

Is Jess right, can we figure out how long a walk should take by timing someone over a short **distance**?

22

PROVE IT!

Find out how fast you walk.
You need:

I 3-foot (1-meter) ruler
I string
I watch with a second hand
I calculator

1

Measure out a 32-feet (about 10-meter) path and lay a piece of string along it.

2

Use the watch to time how long it takes you to walk normally along the path.

Use the calculator to figure out your **speed** by dividing the distance traveled by time. So, if you walk 32 feet (10 m) in 5 seconds, your speed would be: 32 feet (10 m) ÷ 5 seconds = 6.4 feet (2 m) per second.

10 ÷ 5
6 ÷ 2.45

2.45

WHY IT WORKS

In science, it is often useful to know the speed at which something is traveling. We measure speed by working out the distance traveled in a given time. The speed of cars, for example, is often measured in miles or kilometers per hour. If it took you 5 seconds to travel 6 feet, how far would you travel in a minute? What would your speed be, in miles or meters per hour?

VILLAGE
6 MILES

RESCUE!

Just as the friends are arguing, they hear a whirring sound above them.

"Look, it's a helicopter!" says Jess, waving and shouting loudly.

"We've got to get the pilot's attention," says Zac, fighting back tears. "It's our last chance to get back before dark."

"I've got it! My trusty pack saves the day again..." says Ben. "I'll make a mint and cola rocket that he can't miss."

PROVE IT!

You must ask an adult to help you make this fun but explosive rocket. You need:

- tube of mint Mentos candies
- 64-ounce (2-liter) bottle of diet cola
- wide tape
- open space outdoors, like a field

? WHAT DO YOU THINK?

Is Ben right, can you use mints and cola to make a rocket?

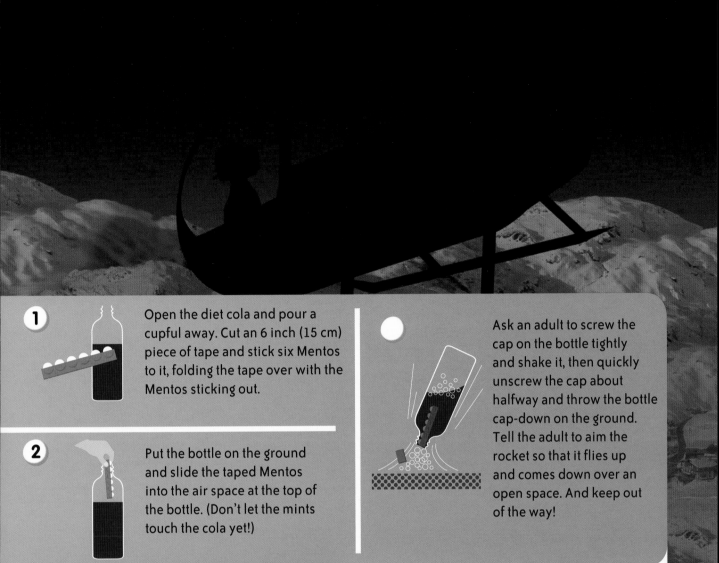

1 Open the diet cola and pour a cupful away. Cut an 6 inch (15 cm) piece of tape and stick six Mentos to it, folding the tape over with the Mentos sticking out.

2 Put the bottle on the ground and slide the taped Mentos into the air space at the top of the bottle. (Don't let the mints touch the cola yet!)

Ask an adult to screw the cap on the bottle tightly and shake it, then quickly unscrew the cap about halfway and throw the bottle cap-down on the ground. Tell the adult to aim the rocket so that it flies up and comes down over an open space. And keep out of the way!

WHY IT WORKS

Shaking Mentos in the diet cola makes tons of bubbles. When the bottle hits the ground, the bubbles blow off the lid. In forces, for every action there is an equal and opposite reaction. When the contents of the "rocket" push downwards, the rocket is **thrusted** upwards!

"Ben, you're a genius," says Amelie, as the pilot signals she's seen them and starts to descend. "I'll never complain about you dragging that backpack around with us again!"

"I'll complain if he doesn't!" says Zac, cheerfully. "Without it we wouldn't be heading home now for a hot chocolate!"

QUIZ

1 Which of these statements is true?

a) Forces make things move.

b) Forces can make things stop moving.

2 What is the force that occurs when objects rub together, and slows down moving objects?

a) gravity

b) friction

c) weight

3 Which of these statements is false?

a) Weight is the pull of friction on objects.

b) Weight is the pull of gravity on objects.

4 Which of these is not a force?

a) friction

b) weight

c) height

5 Which of these statements is true?

a) An object can have only one force acting on it at one time.

b) An object can have several forces acting on it at the same time.

6 What is a lever?

a) a machine that helps you to lift heavy objects using little force

b) the object you are trying to lift

7

What is a fulcrum?

a) the point on which a lever rests or is supported

b) the effort you use to push down on a lever to lift the load

8

Which of these statements is true?

a) Objects with rougher, bumpier surfaces create more friction.

b) Smoother objects and surfaces create less friction.

10

When an object falls, air resistance ...

a) acts in the opposite direction to the movement

b) acts in the same direction as the movement

c) does not act at all

9

What is air resistance?

a) the force of friction caused by air on an object

b) the push that air can give an object so it goes faster

c) the force of air squashing an object

12

Which of these statements is true?

a) The pulling force of magnets on some metals gets weaker over a distance.

b) The pulling force of magnets on some metals gets stronger over a distance.

11

Magnets have two poles. What are they called?

a) North and South

b) West and East

FIND OUT MORE

BOOKS

Gut-Wrenching Gravity and Other Fatal Forces (Disgusting and Dreadful Science)
Anna Claybourne, Franklin Watts, 2013

Hands-On Science: Forces and Motion, Kingfisher, 2013

Investigating Magnetism (How Does Energy Work?)
Sally M. Walker, Lerner Publishing, 2011

Push and Pull: The Science of Forces (Big Bang Science Experiments)
Jay Hawkins, Windmill Books, 2013

Zombies and Forces and Motion (Monster Science)
Mark Weakland, Capstone Press, 2012

WEBSITES

Watch this video to see easy hands-on friction experiments:
https://www.youtube.com/watch?v=24f_cKLJRNY

This website has lots of ideas for experiments and activities using magnets and magnetism:
www.exploratorium.edu/snacks/iconmagnetism.html

Watch videos to learn more about the basics of magnets and magnetism:
www.brainpop.com/science/motionsforcesandtime/magnetism/preview.weml

Help with a friction investigation in the Science Center:
www.pbskids.org/sid/funwithfriction.html

Every effort has been made by the publisher to ensure that these websites contain no inappropriate or offensive material. However, because of the nature of the Internet, it is impossible to guarantee that the content of these sites will not be altered. We strongly advise that Internet access is supervised by a responsible adult.

GLOSSARY

air resistance form of friction between a moving object and the air around it

avalanche sudden rush of lots of snow, ice, or rocks down a mountain

compass instrument that uses a magnetic needle to show direction

distance amount of space between two places or objects

effort force needed by a machine in order to act upon a load

force push or pull that makes an object move, go faster, or change direction

friction force that is caused by contact between the surfaces of two objects, and that slows down movement

fulcrum the point around which a lever turns

gravity force that pulls objects down towards the center of the Earth

lever simple machine that increases force, letting you do a lot of easy work instead of doing a little bit of hard work

load amount of something that is moved by a machine

magnet object or material that attracts iron and some other metals

poles two points, such as the ends of a magnet, that have opposing magnetic qualities

simple machine basic piece of equipment with a system of parts that work together

speed how far something travels in a given amount of time

surface area total area of an exposed surface

thrust force that makes an object move or speed up

weight measure of the pull of gravity on an object

INDEX